UNDER GLASS

poems by

Victoria Woolf Bailey

Finishing Line Press
Georgetown, Kentucky

UNDER GLASS

For Robin

ACKNOWLEDGMENTS

At the Yard Sale originally appeared in the chapbook *Dragging Gunter's Chain* published by Finishing Line Press (2014)

One Man's Trash was published in *The Henderson Community College Literary Magazine* (2014)

A special thanks goes to Bruce Bailey for putting up with me for all these years.

Publisher: Leah Huete de Maines
Editor: Christen Kincaid
Cover Art: Victoria Bailey
Author Photo: Michael Gray, michaelgrayphotography.com
Cover Design: Elizabeth Maines McCleavy

Order online: www.finishinglinepress.com
also available on amazon.com

Author inquiries and mail orders:
Finishing Line Press
PO Box 1626
Georgetown, Kentucky 40324
USA

Table of Contents

*You might see me as a Pied Piper,
playing my flute with a long line of stuff -
old windows and shutters and colorful tins
dancing the conga behind me.*

Aimless

In a tote full of old pictures,
wedding announcements,
and obituaries,
I find a letter
addressed to me
in Sheridan, Wyoming.

I was 23 and far from home.
I know from the date
you will be dead in a few months.
But you didn't know that.
What 42 year-old woman
expects to die?

The next year I moved to Kansas,
the year after that, Ohio,
the year after that, Louisiana,
spent two years in Florida,
then moved to Kentucky.

But there are no letters
addressed to those places,
no one telling me in a beautiful cursive,
*I'm glad to hear you are doing so well
and are happy.*

My Mistake

I could have left
years earlier,
found a better life
and not looked back
except for my parent's
antique furniture, mahogany
from the 1920's
passed down to me,
stored at his mother's house.
The china cabinet,
the carved-back chairs,
the two hutches,
the marble-top table,
all that I had left of home,
all that I had left of them.
And with that hard to move
heaviness he held me hostage
and I did not walk away.

What Robin and I Remember

After thirty years what she remembers
is the pickled poke I brought to her party.

It was the only party we ever went to.
It was only time he hit me.

I carried a baby on my back.
Someone else brought shrimp.

***

I think of Robin as the center of a wheel
with friends like spokes and she tells their stories.

At the top of the Hebbardsville hill,
everyone has a story.

***

I learned about poke when I was a child,
scouring the fields for knowledge, and over the years

I've picked gallons and gallons of blackberries.
One time I picked fourteen ticks from my hair.

***

Before I knew Robin she held a baby in her arms,
warmed only by her warmth until her child grew cold.

After my divorce. she kept me sane. I struggled
to fill the propane tank. At her house there was always food.

***

Robin digs a hole in the woods searching for treasure,
old bottles and broken crocks, leather weathered in the dirt.

They say we are always searching for something we have lost.

***

One year in September spring greens reseeded and grew thick.
I froze lambsquarter, mustard, dock, whatever I could find

to feed my family and spent hours on the concrete porch
cracking black walnuts and the pecans from Robin's yard.

She only keeps the ancient—bottles, blown and corked,
shovel reaching deeper into the past we all share.

***

After his divorce, Robin's neighbor leaves a heap
of charred ruins near the hole where she digs.

She finds broken dolls and figurines, piles porcelain heads
into buckets and drags them into the house.

I admire her vintage pottery bought for pennies
at yard sales, years ago, when her friends were buying diapers.

***

I haven't had poke in years. Yesterday an old woman
told me she fries hers in bacon grease.

I'll have to try that. At the edge of my yard
bright red stalks still grow, topped with purple berries.

Some weeds I never pull and ditch lilies line the woods,
their tubers a hidden treasure stored against want.

***

They say bottles are more valuable
after they have been underground, after they have been ruined.

Their sheen becomes a dull rainbow
revealing their age and authenticity.

***

The problem with poke is its poison,
a powerful cathartic that must be leeched.

I boiled the stalks and drained twice, used the pickle mix
that comes in packets at Rural King.

The directions call for cucumbers
but I used what I had.

***

Now several years have passed since I made it to Robin's house,
a museum full of dusty artifacts and spoiled dogs.

Today, when I visit, her yard is full of chickens and stray cats.
When I pull in the driveway, roosters crow.

The Monster

Years ago I had a rule.
I would never pack a moving box
bigger than I myself could carry
but I never had much
as I wondered from state to state.

Then came five feet of antique mahogany,
an inheritance full of memories
too heavy for me to move alone.
I called it the monster
but oh, what it could hold!

A small drawer on either side,
two pull-open cupboards,
and in the middle, the huge belly of the beast
that I fattened with found treasures—
old Pyrex, hammered aluminum,

vintage costume jewelry,
the many things I brought home
to keep me from going hungry.

At the Yard Sale

I never should have stopped
but how was I to know what was buried
in that box of picture frames. The woman said,
I'll let you have the whole thing for five dollars.

I ask about the people in the photos.
She shrugs.
I ask her where she got all the stuff.
She looks away and says something vague.

We hear about disasters far away,
watch people try to salvage what they can
after the big blow. But here
there is no telling how it happened,
things left in storage with no way to pay
are auctioned off to the highest bidder.

And there in a box, mixed with old bestsellers,
I spot yearbooks from the county high,
find my son smiling in his senior picture
next to the girl whose name is engraved on the cover.

I hear the woman tell her friend, *One time
I opened a box and found someone's nursing license.*
She takes another drag and stares into space.
Her husband lowers the price on a big screen TV.
I look into the eyes of a laughing baby,
agonize over the caption *Mommy and Me.*

One Man's Trash

A few years ago, I hauled some old windows
home from the Dumpster on Boswell Road.
They are still leaned up in the shed
covered with cobwebs and spiders.
I meant to do something with them.
We always mean to do a thing and plan it out
but whether it's really going to happen
we need a crystal ball to discern.
But I don't believe in stuff like Quji boards,
tarot cards or horoscopes. But I do believe in windows,
the kind I see at craft shows, whitewashed frames,
panes replaced with stained glass,
and I reason in all my manic delusions- *I could do that!*

If You Go to Robin's House

You will see the goats and chickens,
the cats who will perch on your car,
the dogs large and small.
You will marvel at glass doorknobs,
hand embroidered linens, ceramics from another era.
But I tell you – it is not enough.

In order to understand, you must climb
to the attic, gaze at the cracked porcelain face
glued among the decorative tiles.
You must see the dolls in the basement,
arms, legs, and broken heads stored in separate containers.
Even then, it is not enough. It will never be enough.

Framed

Here was a real picture of real people
and I felt guilty. Well, vaguely uncomfortable.
It was a beautiful frame and I wanted it bad enough
to put out of my mind these nice-looking
people trapped under glass and stuck with a dollar
price tag. The woman, if I had to guess, was probably a nurse,
the husband a firefighter or maybe a football coach.
The baby, obviously a girl, had no hair but I really wanted the frame
and wouldn't you know when I took it apart there were names
on the back and a date: Rob, Paula and Katie, 12/27/95.
Maybe the picture got thrown out with the rest of his stuff
after his last affair or maybe his step-grandmother died
and no one here cares about Rob, Paula and Katie
living way up in Alaska, at least not as much as I do
and I wonder where Katie is now and how she has fared
since the divorce. And I think I will keep them, like distant
relatives, all in my prayers.

After They Remodeled

In the alley between two brick buildings
I found a long panoramic from the 1933
automobile insurance salesmen's convention,
white men in gray suits with hats in their hands
and in the front row, four women bundled
against the November cold in coats
with large fur collars. And I realized
they are all dead and that's how it is—
one moment life's a party, friends laugh,
and pose for pictures but then they go their way
and the only thing left is a black and white photo
hung on the wall of an insurance company
in a brick building downtown, then tossed in the alley
when there is no one who remembers,
and no one can say what really happened.

The Prolific

Some of the critics expressed the opinion that he wrote too much.
—*Otto A Rothert "The Story of a Poet: Madison Cawein"*

He was German-blooded, Kentucky born,
and this thick green volume, rescued from a cart
marked *free* at the Henderson County Public Library,
compares his work to that of Keats and Coleridge.
He was a lover of nature, filling notebook after notebook
in the solitude of Iroquois Park, sitting on stone steps
carved by rushing water. But where is he now?
Cloistered on shelves seldom seen, his name known only
in the halls of academia or stumbled upon
by collectors of discarded treasure.

Hoarding Words

Sometimes it starts with sap flowing,
a five-gallon bucket of embarrassment that boils
until there is nothing left but dark sayings.

Often there is a struggle, a journey
with no map, old plats insisting
the corners are marked with iron pins.

Sometimes there are dreams,
bikinis of meaning
tossed like shells on the beach.

Always there is the sun, a whore cleaned up
and gone to church only to find
again, the darkness.

Plants and rocks, pinecones and seeds.
Books, so many books.
Sometimes it is all too much.

Number Three Thousand and Fifty-One

Rocks and bones
shells   and papers,
plastic totes, and books   and files
tins and pictures,   and beads   and pearls,
empty vases. frames   and scissors ,   film and pens,
notes,   and bells,   and boxes,   bears and candles,
and lamps,   vintage tins and vintage maps
vintage keys, coats and scarves and rings
and pretty and pretty and old and lovely
and lots and lots of stuff and s tuff a n d st uff.

Defectibility

At the farm auction I bought a set of shelves
layered with china plates, crystal, and every kind
of glassware—stuff stored in a dusty basement—
shiny objects covered with spiderwebs and grime.

I brought them home, ran dishes
through a sink of soapy water and found
what no one had seen: the sparkle of cut glass,
the beauty of years past.

I am always looking for what others have missed—
the small coin of great value, a plain pebble
adorned by an ancient fossil,
the perfect word to describe my obsession.

Broken

There's a broken prism
on the windowsill,
reflecting a broken
rainbow, as the sun
moves across
my broken sky.

No telling how
it happened or why.
But I keep it there
with its cracked base,
upside down,
in a place of honor.

Ditch Lilies

Who knew you could stuff the buds with cheese?
I thought I knew how to digest wild things,
mushrooms and other harbingers   of what?
My friend at the nursing home is out of her mind,
plays with brightly colored blocks and insists
she wants to go home. She worries
about her mother who may or may not
be alive. The easy answer is not always yes.

Some people cram French fries
into their mouths and worry about their weight.
Sometimes it's hard to say no.

Eve Offers an Apple

I saw an empty fruitcake tin,
made in Germany, with a built-in music box
but could tell from the bar code on the bottom
it wasn't old but deceptively decorated
with an ivory-necked cameo that caught my eye.
But I thought better of it and left it on the shelf
with its thrift store tag and its painted lady
still whispering *Come hither.*

Close Call

She could take the arrangement
apart. She could use
the flowers and bow.
She could put the whole thing
in the trunk of the car
while passing through
a nice neighborhood
on trash day.

She could leave it later
in a shopping cart
when she comes to her senses
in a parking lot.

Among All the Clutter

I find a picture of myself in a baby carriage
asleep next to a stuffed animal and instantly
recognize that face though now sandblasted by the years.

Some mornings I scare myself in the mirror,
the wild hair I've always had
and I notice that baby's unruly curls.

Was she dreaming? What could have filled
her thoughts when the file cabinet of the mind
was not stuffed full, covered like every flat surface
within reach of my grown-up self?

Dead or Alive

I've brought home another picture
of someone I don't know, a boy
about four, wearing a suit
and I think he would be about my age
judging by the style of clothes
and the tinted portrait. But where is he now?
Maybe he is sitting at a desk writing
about his childhood, the poverty
his family fell into, the reasons
his pictures were scattered and found
by a stranger who liked the frame,
while I sit here writing about nature,
watch the squirrels out my window
gather and bury acorns and the vultures
circling another dead possum.

My Big-Eyed Girls

I bought them at a yard sale.
Bell-bottoms and peasant blouses
hint at the decade they were popular.

Who doesn't love a big-eyed girl?

And who doesn't wish
they could still sport the dewiness of youth,
the look of surprise
hidden behind those painted eyes?

Smoke

The picture of us in front of the Grand Tetons
was a mirage, the hitchhiking story I've always told,
a highway built on smoke and mirrors.

The door is open. The door is never open.
I read an essay about a house with no door.

Daffodils bloom each spring then hide
themselves underground. I suddenly realize
why those prints on the wall are so important.

Those images of big-eyed girls and my daughters,
set side by side, nothing but paper and paint.
Tell me my children made it out alive.

Thirst

Sometimes my nerves go bare like winter
trees that spread underground
in a mirror image of cold pain.
And to think—in a few months, heat
will force us to find a shady place.
And which is better—the destruction of evil
or the warmth we crave that breeds the bugs
we will curse as they bite and drink our blood?

I think I will have to write my own obituary
if I don't want the flowery praise and exaggeration
of a well-meaning friend or relative
who doesn't know each fault intimately,
the half-empty glass I drink as I dream of waterfalls,
the warmth of a hot spring, and wonder
about my tremendous thirst.

In the Place Where I Sit

I wait for a pinprick of light
to shine through the eastern trees.

How many mornings I've waited
at different hours as earth's clock

moves slowly through the seasons.
Frogs croak in the spring, the cicadas

in summer, the long silent winter
pierced by the caw of a crow

and the falling snow, a disturbed branch
giving up its captured beauty.

And still I am here, safe behind glass,
safe from heat and the sweat of humidity,

safe from the sting of cold reddened
cheeks. But even here I am touched

by a chill breeze sneaking through
windows of a house that once was new.

Mahogany

I was finally ready to let them go,
the too-big pieces of my family's history,
taking up space in a house too small
for a formal dining room.
And the lady who paints furniture,
distressed, in the current style,
gave me cash, loaded them in her truck
and hauled them away.
I kept them too long but now I am free,
memories of mahogany, a painful veneer
not as thick as I had imagined.

Salvage City

It all ends up here, every memory,
every dream, gutters,

old washing machines,
slate from a mansion's roof,

a baby carriage, a wooden leg,
a windshield broken by a head.

a diner built to be hauled into place,
round stools and memories of teenage floats,

stingray bikes, all kinds of boats,
the space shuttle ride from in front of a store,

the car you drove right out of school,
everyone's favorite rusty tool,

a life-sized pirate, a carnival game,
complete with a hammer, the bell at the top.

It's all the same, an axe, a shovel,
a headless mop,

the end of every dream and life,
piled and jumbled, covered with rust

comes to this place
on its way to dust.

In the Old Hoarder's Apartment

I searched
for the beeping,
checked the alarm clock,
the smoke detector,
the oxygen.

I found it
hidden
under the bed,
a brass timepiece
in a thrift shop bag,
chiming.

Victoria Woolf Bailey grew up in New Jersey, spent several years traveling all over the county and lived in eight different states before finding the home of her dreams on a small piece of land in rural Kentucky. She has been a member of Green River Writers in Louisville for many years and is thankful for all the wonderful poets she has met along the way.

Her work has appeared in a number of publications including: *The Post Grad Journal, Jelly Bucket, Pine Mountain Sand & Gravel* and the *Tipton Poetry Journal*. She is the author of a previous chapbook, *Dragging Gunter's Chain* (Finishing Line Press 2014) and a full-length collection, *Cannibalism and the Copenhagen Interpretation: a Love Story*, published by Finishing Line Press in 2022.